DRAMATIC ELEMENTS IN AMERICAN INDIAN CEREMONIALS

By Virginia Shropshire Heath

"Poetry in general," says Aristotle, "seems to have sprung from two causes, each of them lying deep in our nature—first, the instinct of imitation . . ., next, . . . the instinct for 'harmony' and 'rhythm.'" Many of the lyric-legend-dance complexes of certain North American Indian religious ceremonials would seem to bear out this judgment. Indeed, in not a few of the unmistakably poetic expressions, there may be found well-defined dramatic elements suggesting the possibility of a developed, independent dramatic literature, had these savage peoples been left alone to initiate a civilization and culture of their own. The South American Indians were capable of evolving a secular form of drama, as Sir Clements Markham affirms on the strength of the romantic "Ollantay" of the Incas of Peru. Certainly the North American Indians, many of whom were superior in religious conceptions and practices to their more civilized kindred of the south, could have equalled if not surpassed them in the matter of dramatic expression. For the peoples of the north, the idea of religion, of genuine worship, still lay at the root of all dramatic production. Hence, out of the great admixture of savage love of song, of story, and of rhythm, heightened by religious terrors and spiritual yearnings, must be sifted the mimetic actions and speeches fundamental to the drama proper, especially to serious drama; for to the savage mind, Nature, in one conception or another, the great dispenser of the necessities as well as of the "good things" of life, is a matter of deadly earnest.

It is the red man's promise of a finished dramatic literature unaffected by the white man's tampering that constitutes my reason for investigating the ancient religious ceremonials of a limited number of Indian linguistic stocks.[1] The interplay of tribal influences presents complications enough in any of the religious types known among the American Indians north of Mexico. The type represented by the pueblo, the great plains, and eastern woodland peoples, alone affords dramatic material of enormous proportions. In defining this type Dr. Boas[2] says:

> The principal characteristic of the mythologies of the area of the great plains, the eastern woodlands, and the arid southwest is the tendency to a systematization of the myths under the influence of a highly developed ritual.

In this great religious attempt at the rationalization of the universe and its powers is sounded the keynote of the more distinctly human institution, dramatic art, the basic function of which is an explanation of and a judgment upon human events and human destinies.

Within the confines of this one type arise differentiations that tend to segregate the pueblo type of ceremonial from that of the plains and the eastern woodlands. Among the former, the idea of dramatic action has progressed so far as to subordinate the ritual side of the ceremonial, while among the latter the predominance of the ritual leaves comparatively small scope for the display of action. Thus, according to Mr. Miller's interpretation[3] of the essentials of the drama—namely, speech and action—within the confines of this one type of religious ceremonial appear two separate and distinct sorts of treatment. The pueblo performance would tend to degenerate into pantomime; the plains and eastern woodland ceremonial might relapse into lyric or epic recitals. But this condition of affairs is in no sense necessary. The

---

[1] *Iroquoian*—Seneca, Onondaga Huron; *Algonquian*—Ojibwa, Arapaho, Cheyenne; *Siouan*—Dakota, Omaha, Winnebago; *Caddoan*—Pawnee; *Shoshonean*—Hopi (Pueblo); *Athapascan*—Navajo. For geographical distribution, especially of last four stocks named, see map of linguistic families of North America—Bureau of American Ethnology, Bulletin 30, Part I, Washington, 1906.

[2] Bureau of American Ethnology, Bul. 30, art. "Religion."

[3] Miller, *Dramatic Elements in Popular Ballad;* University Studies, University of Cincinnati, 1905.

second possibility is scarcely worth noting; for, the dramatic conception once realized, it is not likely to lose ground. Music, sung ritual, together with rhythmic motion, aside from certain stage settings, help to retain in the epic-lyric nature of the plains tribes' ceremonials, distinct dramatic features. On the other hand, the religious or ritual content is almost as generally understood by the pueblo audience as were the accepted plots of classic tragedy which were the common property of the Greek audience. Whereas the Greek went to hear the poets' ideas upon certain human situations, the Indian of the pueblo type went to see how the members of the various societies would act in the rôle of gods or other supernatural beings. From the standpoint of his savage interest, dialogue is, in the main, non-essential. Songs and musical accompaniment fulfil at least in part the general function of dialogue.

PUEBLO CEREMONIALS

Of the religious observances in which dramatic action predominates, some of the best instances may be cited among the Hopi or Moki, distinctly a pueblo people, and the Navajo, a pueblo-influenced people. Both the purely communal and the largely individual ceremonials are celebrated by each of these tribes; but for the sake of definiteness, let us first review two of the Hopi indoor performances, Katcina impersonations, as they are called, both of a communal nature; and later, take up a Navajo celebration of the individual sort.

In considering the dramatic features of ceremonials among pueblo, plains, and eastern woodland peoples, it must be remembered that sympathetic magic constitutes the very backbone of all drama-like performances. Not even among the pueblo tribes have the most spectacular of shows freed themselves from this religious content. All have as their basic purpose the influencing of supernatural powers or deities, inducing them to grant to otherwise helpless man the various good things of life—peace, plenty, and increase. The celebrations themselves conform strictly to certain fixed codes, subject to little alteration. It is this conformity to the general trend of cosmic and universal myths which in time develops what may be termed texts; for the nature and succes-

sion of these rituals in any given ceremonial, though transmitted
in most cases by word of mouth, take on all the permanent characteristics of the parts and accompanying cues of the recognized
play, with the added emphasis of divinely inflicted punishment
for any failure to give an accurate performance. And yet with
all the fixed nature of the rituals, there is a certain latitude for
individual interpetation which, little by little, becomes embodied
in the form of the rituals themselves. Especially is there license
of this sort among the pueblo Indians. Primarily, however, all
shows are inaugurated to entertain and to propitiate a divine or
supernatural audience rather than for the pleasure of the tangible
body of spectators helping to create the genuinely theatrical atmosphere of inspiration.

Among the Hopi, certain of the Katcina ceremonials offer no
end of interesting material for investigation, especially the so-
called complete or masked Katcina performances. Those playing
Katcina parts are impersonating divine beings, primarily spirits
of the ancients of the Hopi, of such an order as can be represented by men. During the impersonations, the actors by virtue
of their highly symbolic paraphernalia, especially masks, would
seem to become the exalted beings themselves, so intense is the
degree of such acting. Within certain bounds, to judge from the
great diversity existing between Hopi myths and Hopi dramatic
representations, both individuals and companies have possessed
themselves of unexpected license in the matter of interpretation
and presentation of fixed rôles. "Conservatism in dress," to
quote Mr. Fewkes, "is tenaciously adhered to in religious paraphernalia among all peoples." This is as true of the purely religion-dominated performances of the American Indians as it was
true of the semi-secularized dramatic plays of the Greeks.

Hopi Representations

Soyáluña

Of the elaborate or complete Katcinas, few offer better material
for investigation than certain portions of the Soyáluña, the warrior's observance, sometimes called the " Return Katcina," for it

celebrates the return of the sun, the god of war as well as the god of germination.   This religious observance occurs in December at the time of the winter solstice and serves, it would seem, as a sort of invocation to the sun, an insurance of its return.   There are many preliminary ceremonials, as there are in all such religious celebrations.   These occur in the various *kivas*, secret society lodges, previous to the final central dramatization which takes place on the last night in the Moñkiva.

To get a clear idea of this distinctly indoor performance, imagine yourself a companion of Mr. Fewkes for the celebration of 1891 at Walpi.[4]   Upon entering the *kiva* or secret society lodge through the hatchway,[5] perhaps the first thing to be noticed would be the bower effect of the ceiling, so studded is it with numerous strands of feathers and piñon needles, each strand, by the way, having played an important symbolic part in the period of preparation.   At the west wall of the kiva is an altar of stacked corn flanked and fronted by a bank of shrubbery, the space between the corn pile and the roof being filled with wands ornamented with artificial flowers.   In the center of the shrubbery facing east, is a gourd with an eight inch aperture through which is thrust the head of an effigy of Paliiliikoñuh, the plumed-headed snake of the type certain of the Katcinas brought with them as pets, when first they emerged upon the upper earth through the *sípapû*, or opening in the center of the earth.   The head of this effigy is painted black.   A tongue-like appendage hangs from its mouth.   All the preliminary chants and dances, in which various kiva groups may be distinguished, each with its own type of head covering or mask, decorated with symbols of rain clouds (an almost constant prayer among these desert folk is the prayer for rain), and each with its characteristic sun-shield,—all these may be passed over for the sake of the ceremony proper which comprises a purely religious rite followed by a performance of religious import, unmistakably dramatic in character.

On the north side of the room is seated one old chief alone and,

4 See 15th *Annual Report of the Bureau of Ethnology,* Washington, 1897.
5 See Pl. IV, 19th *A. R. B. E.,* Washington, 1898.   The pueblo kiva is underground, hence the hatchway.

opposite him on the south, sit twelve chiefs, the floor space between being clear. The gorgeously arrayed novices from the various other kivas, each carrying imitation squash blossoms and spruce twigs in the left hand and corn in the right, approaching the twelve chiefs over an especially strewn path of sand, squat before them, facing south. The old chief on the north crosses the room and takes his seat at the east of the line of chiefs. When all are assembled, kiva members and outside spectators standing against the eastern wall, the priests take their places before the altar. After a moment of intensely solemn quiet, the officiating priest casts a handful of meal towards the effigy and says a short prayer, quite likely to some unseen power rather than to the effigy itself. Then, as if in recognition of this offering, the head of the snake, quivering, seems to rise of itself slowly to the center of the opening in the gourd. At this point, it seems to give vent to four short melodious roars, after which it again subsides to its former position. Following this may be heard a scraping sound, then all is quiet. Thereafter, each chief follows the example of the priest with a like result.

At this point, the public nature of the ceremony seems completed, for all the uninitiated spectators leave the kiva. The intensely dramatic conflict taking place at this juncture is for the most part private, only the Moñkiva members constituting any sort of fixed audience. One chief, wearing the mask and bearing the sun-shield characteristic of his kiva, advances and declaims in a half chant, rising to a shriek at intervals. During this recital he draws back to the fire-place and then shuffles slowly toward the *sípapû,* an opening in the floor symbolizing the original opening in the center of the earth through which the Katcinas came with the Indians. At this point, the Moñkiva chief shouts loudly and the chief on the verge of the *sípapû* springs over that opening, after which all shout and sing in concert.

The associates of the chief now taking the leading part, dash down the ladder into the main room each bearing the sun-shield distinctive of his kiva. Each of the band presents his shield to his chief in military fashion. Then, except for the two members, novices likely, who stand facing each other against the north wall, bearing in the right hand a squash blossom and spruce twigs and in the left an ear of corn, the whole company engages in a frenzied dance in which the chief makes mad dashes among his associates, who, crouching, meets his assaults and drive him back to the *sípapû*. He swings his shield and dashes it from face to face, all in perfect unison, those so attacked pretending to snatch at it. The whole performance, highly suggestive of defense and attack, is kept up until those participating are overcome with heat and exhaustion, the chief shield-bearer alone triumphing.

So much for the dramatic spectacle. The rituals accompanying and accounting for the action remain obscure to the alien spectator. In view of this, perhaps it will not be amiss to note the salient features of Mr. Fewkes's purely theoretic interpretation. This assault of men upon the bearer of the sun-shield may be taken as a dramatization of the attacks of hostile powers upon the sun-god himself. The object of this act is perhaps to offset the malign influences or to overcome them through suggestion, for it will be remembered that the shield-bearer, though made to retreat to the *sípapû,* is never overcome by his assailants. All this is done to bring back the vegetation-fostering sun, lest he disappear forever as seems threatened by his southern decline. This probably constitutes the central motive of the entire enactment. But before this can be made effective, first must one of the oldest and most powerful of the sun's enemies be propitiated. It is on this account that prayers are said to the Plumed Snake. It is with this in view that meal offerings are made to the would-be devastator of the earth, should he succeed in banishing Táwa, the beneficent sun. When the Plumed Snake has been won over, then may the bearer of the symbolic sun-shield of Táwa assure, through successful fighting, the return of that good friend of man.

Paliiliikoñti

The Soyáluña exhibition does not, however, merit the consideration due some other Hopi ceremonials. The Paliiliikoñti, for example, presents a far more markedly dramatic show. The vaudeville-like performances, coming as a climax to this celebration, fulfill all the conditions attendant upon place, audience, and representative rôles.

The Paliiliikoñti or Plumed Snake ceremonial, occurring in March, has for its basic purpose the production of rain, the Plumed Snake being associated with lightning. Sympathetic magic is operative in the propitiatory treatment accorded the great serpent effigies, employed in the final dramatic performances. The suggestion of crop-producing rains is further emphasized upon this occasion in stage paraphernalia of various kinds; for instance, young shoots of corn. Each show constitutes in itself an independent unit, each being the product of a separate kiva. All, however, voice the central theme of the entire Paliiliikoñti observance, a desire for rain and subsequent crops, especially corn. An account of the first, the fourth, and the fifth acts, as presented in the various kivas on the East Mesa in 1890, will give an idea of the general nature of these dramatizations.[6]

One end of the kiva was arranged for seating the audience, the other side being reserved as stage space for the various transient companies of actors and their stage paraphernalia. The fireplace in the center of the room served as a dividing line as well as the source of illumination. The fire-tenders, too, performed a double function. Their primary duty was to replenish the fire, thereby providing general light for the room or foot-lights as the occasion demanded. Their secondary duty was that of official curtain. When scene-shifting was under way, the two fire-tenders created temporary darkness by shutting off all light with their robes. When all was in readiness for the exhibition, at a given signal the robes were dropped and the stage setting and actors were revealed. With this introduction to the theater, the management of the theater, and the audience, the shows themselves may be brought on.

[6] See 21st *A. R. B. E.*, Washington, 1912. *Proc. Acad. Sci.*, December; 1900; "The Palulakonti: A Tusayan Ceremony," *Journ. Am. Folk Lore*, 1893.

Act I

The arrival of the first band of Katcina impersonators was announced by strange cries from the hatchway. After repeated summons from the fire-tenders to enter, the actors descended the ladder, in the protecting darkness afforded them by the fire-tenders in their capacity of curtain, and set up their scenic effects. When all was in readiness, the fire-tenders dropped their robes, so revealing to the audience a miniature cornfield against a cloth screen background extending from the floor almost to the rafters. On this were many strange devices, most prominent among which were six large disks encircled by corn husk wreaths and decorated with symbolic pictures of the sun. On other parts of the screen were many symbols of the male and female elements in nature, ranging from birds to human beings together with symbols of rain clouds, lightning, and falling rain. In the foreground on each side of the screen were men representing bear Katcinas in ceremonial kilts, one of whom was dressed to represent a woman. The latter bore in one hand a basket tray of meal and in the other an ear of corn. He wore a black helmet in which were cut small crescent-shaped eyes. On each side of the face coils of hair were suspended and over the forehead hung red horsehair bangs. From the top of the mask protruded a bunch of feathers. This was an impersonation of Hahaiwüpti, mother of Katcinas.

The act began with a song to the rhythm of which all except Hahaiwüpti danced. While this song was still in progress, a hoarse roar was heard from behind the screen, and shortly thereafter the disks swung open and out of the orifices protruded the heads of six great serpent effigies—goggle eyes, a fan-shaped crest of hawk feathers, and a mouth with prominent teeth from which hung a red leather tongue. The bodies, thrust slowly into view, were black on the back and white on the under side. When they were fully extended, the song grew louder and faster. The effigies, swaying to the rhythm, seemed to bite at each other and to make frequent darts towards the men near the screen. Then the heads of the serpents suddenly turned towards the floor and in an instant the effigies had swept across the imitation cornfield, overturning the little clay pedestals to which the corn shoots were attached.   After this all six serpents raised their heads and wagged them back and forth, roaring continually in spite of all Hahai-wüpti's efforts to appease them.   In the audience as on the stage, wild excitement prevailed.   Some of the spectators threw meal at the effigies, others said prayers, others shouted aimlessly.

At length the song diminished in volume, the effigies disappeared through their respective orifices, the sun disks fell into place, and, after one final roar from behind the screen, all was quiet.   The miniature corn stalks were distributed in the audience, after which the actors packed up their possessions, in the semi-darkness provided by the fire-tenders, and set out for the next kiva where they were to repeat this self-same act.

Act IV

Again strange cries were heard from the hatchway and again the fire-tenders found it necessary several times to bid the visitors enter.   At length, there came down the ladder a man wearing a mask covered with vertical zigzag lines.   On his back he carried a bundle which seemed to be very heavy for he pretended to slip on every rung of the ladder as he descended   When he finally reached the floor he opened the bundle and displayed a metate and meal-grinding stone.   These he arranged before the fire-place and then seated himself to one side.   Another man followed similarly laden, and disposed of the contents of his bundle in like manner, seating himself upon the opposite side.   Now came two masked girls elaborately dressed in white ceremonial blankets and knelt before the grinding stones in the attitude of those about to grind corn.   At this point a chorus of masked men entered and took their places behind the girls.   Then, to the rhythm of a solemn dance, the men began to sing, further complicating the rhythm by clapping their hands.   Meanwhile, swaying their bodies to the basic rhythm of the song, the girls ground corn.

When this scene was completed, the young men in the rôle of brothers to the girls grinding corn, carried on an animated conversation with the fire-tenders relative to the reputation of the girls as grinders.   By way of convincing both the fire-tenders and even certain members of the audience of the truth of their statements, the chorus presented them with pinches of meal to taste.

At the conclusion of this episode, the girls performed a graceful dance in the middle of the room, extending alternately their hands in which they carried ears of corn.[7]

Act V

The general scenic features of this act were similar to those already described in the first act, the main difference being the wooden background decorated with turkey feathers and providing only two sun disks.   Pine boughs filled the spaces at the sides of the screen, serving to conceal the manipulators of the serpent effigies.   The *dramatis personae* of this act were, however, entirely different from those referred to in the first act.   These actors are to be designated as " mud-heads," intended to be ridiculous figures and to play undignified parts.   Except for the mask of closely fitting cloth with a knob over each ear, slits for eyes and nose, and a doughtnut-like protrusion for a mouth, each actor was naked.   This show, too, began with roars from behind the screen, after which the two great serpents made their appearance much in the same manner as did the six in Act I.   Once in the foreground, they entered into conflicts with the mud-heads whom they always succeeded in overcoming, symbolic of the struggle of man, an ignoble being, with the supernatural power represented by the Great Snake.

This is enough to demonstrate that the Hopi are capable of producing at least semi-secular dramatic performances.   Each act stands for a number of rehearsals with a view to public presentation.   Each show gives striking evidence of the existence of a certain kind of text upon which the exhibition is based.   Even more than the Soyáluña dramatization, the three acts paraphrased from the Paliiliikoñti exhibition demonstrate that the Hopi dra-

[7] Rôle of these girls suggestive of corn maidens in Zuñi mythology. See 23d *A. R. B. E.,* Washington, 1905.

matic conception has progressed beyond the choral stage. The specific character impersonation of the mother of Katcinas is proof of this. And a further instance of the requisites of the secular drama is found in the dialogue between the chorus of young men in Act IV and the fire-tenders. Nor does this exhaust the claims to recognition from a dramatic standpoint. The pervading atmosphere of religious terror in Act I may be compared with that of Greek tragedy; or, barring the religious element, it is certainly suggestive of opera. Greatly tempered in the still more or less serious representations of Act IV, this tragic atmosphere is finally reduced almost to the comic in the mud-head performance of Act V. Again, in both the Soyáluña and Paliilii-koñti ceremonials, the presence of the altar—represented in the latter by the symbolic screen—calls to mind a similar characteristic of the classic Greek stage. And the further analogy of conventional masks and costumes, entirely different though the Indian conventions are from the Greek, nevertheless stimulates a desire to follow out a more detailed comparison of the developed drama of that cultured people with the crude beginnings of drama among this savage folk. Such an investigation, it seems, could but confirm the dramatic promise of certain pueblo ceremonials.

A Navajo Performance

A contrast to the general or communal pueblo ceremonials may be found in " The Mountain Chant " of the pueblo-influenced Navajo. Upon the last night of this protracted medicine ceremonial, instituted for the " cure " of an individual member of the tribe, occurs a dramatic pageant of no mean proportions. In spite of the distinctly individual cast of the celebration as a whole, the performances taking place upon this last night, bear the stamp of a wide-spread festal occasion, involving at least representatives from many other tribes. Those making up the audience bring all the holiday freshness of spirit that the Greeks did upon similar occasions of great dramatic interest. Over all is the powerful element of religion, superstition or whatever you choose to call that profound supernatural influence basic to intense love of action, of story, and above all of mystery.   In this respect, the savage perhaps differs from the more sophisticated Greek almost as much as do the respective times chosen for their great festivals of this sort.   The Greek developed tragedy was presented in all the clarity of day; the Navajo acted legend occurs at night with all the possibilities of mystery and magic which darkness affords. The Navajo is still a savage with the full quota of wild savage love of color, of riotous music, and above everything else of action.   He must see, hear, and feel the *story*.   That is the main thing.   He is not yet ready for calm philosophizing.   To him the universe *is* and he would see and see again *how* it came to be so, not *why*.   Hence it may be of interest to parallel sections of the legend with the acted representations.   Artistotle's *unity of action* is an unheard of, an unrealizable dictum in the Navajo *unity of man* principle of dramatic composition.   It is the various episodes in the supernatural experiences of their great medicine prophet Dsilyi' Neyáni that they come to see upon the last night of "The Mountain Chant."   There is but little coherence, much less unity, existing between the many strange legendary exhibitions, a veritable string of almost unrelated events.   But "the play's the thing."

At nightfall the theater is constructed—ceremonially, it must be remembered, for religion is back of all this celebration, a religion almost top-heavy with symbolism and magic.   In the center of the open space there has been previously heaped a great pile of dry juniper and cedar wood.   Along the circumference of this great circle the men and boys construct the mystic enclosure with heaps of branches, while, to a rattle accompaniment, the old chanter sings the essential song.   This completed, the place of exhibition becomes *sacred ground* which can be entered only through an opening facing the east.   Through this sole gateway the audience file with their temporary camping outfits and establish themselves next to the branch enclosure.   This is the human audience.   Outside the fence is the supernatural audience—the spirits of bears, for instance, and various other ancestral gods. No human being dares encroach upon this privileged space.

When the spectators are settled and it is well dark, the band of musicians whose business it is to furnish the emotional atmosphere throughout the entire series of performances, enter and take their places near the outer edge of the enclosure towards the west. As they begin to play, the great fire in the center is lighted and the exhibition is at hand—a series of shows, which, according to Dr. Matthews[8] whose account is employed, hold the attention and even intense interest of white man and Indian alike.

"THE MOUNTAIN CHANT"

Mythological Basis

This exhibition is not founded upon any immediate experience of or revelation to the prophet Dsilyi' Neyáni (Reared-within-the-Mountain) during his sojourn among the *cigìni* (supernatural beings), but was introduced by a stranger tribe of guests from the south present at the first great Mountain Chant inaugurated by the Navajo *shaman* or medicine man upon the return of the prophet, for the sake of further "purifying" him that he might no longer find "the odors of the lodge...intolerable." Hence, the Mountain Chant was not originated by the prophet, a "healing dance within the dark corral" having long been practised. But it was "imperfect" and needed the supplements Dsilyi' Neyáni was prepared to give from his revelations to render it "the great dance it is now among the Navajo." The dance described in the opposite column has, it is seen, no direct bearing upon the "rites of the dark circle" and yet it is probably never omitted.

Dramatic Representation

First Dance

"When the fire gave out its most intense heat, a warning whistle was heard in the outer darkness, and a dozen forms, lithe and lean, dressed only in the narrow white breech-cloth and moccasins, and daubed with white earth until they seemed a group of living marbles, came bounding through the entrance, yelping like wolves and slowly moving around the fire. As they advanced in single file they threw their bodies into divers attitudes—some graceful, some strained and difficult, some menacing. Now they faced the east, now the south, the west, the north, bearing aloft their slender wands tipped with eagle down. . . . Their course around the fire was to the left, that is, from the east to the west by way of the south and back again to the east by way of the north (a course taken by all the dancers of the night, the order never being reversed). When they had encircled the fire twice, they began to thrust their wands toward it, and it soon became evident that their object was to burn off the tips of eagle down; but, owing to the intensity of the heat, it was difficult to accomplish this, or at least they acted well the part of striving against such difficulty. . . . Many were the unsuccessful attempts; but, at length one by one,

[8] See 5th *A. R. B. E.*, Washington, 1883–1884. For "Original Texts and Translations of Songs," see p. 455.

they all succeeded in burning the downy balls from the ends of their wands. As each accomplished this feat, it became his next **duty to** restore the ball of down [a juggler's trick]. When he succeeded, he held his wand up in triumph, yelped and rushed out of the corral."

Second Dance

"After an interval of three quarters of an hour, the dance of the *kátso-yisçàn*, the great plumed arrow, the potent healing ceremony of the night, began. There were but two performers. They were dressed and arrayed like the *akáninili* ['meal sprinkler' frequently acting in the capacity of sacred messenger], but they bore no meal bags, wore no beaver collars and the parts of their bodies that were not painted black—legs and forearms—were daubed with white earth. Instead of the wand of the *akáninili*, each bore in his hand one of the great plumed arrows. While they were making the usual circuits around the fire, the patient was placed, sitting on a buffalo robe in front of the orchestra. They halted before the patient; each dancer seized his arrow between his thumb and fore-finger about eight inches from the tip, held the arrow up to view, giving a coyote-like yelp, as if to say, 'So far will I swallow it' and then appeared to thrust the arrow slowly and painfully down his throat as far as indicated. While the arrows seemed still to be stuck in their throats, they danced a 'chassé, right and left' with short, shuffling steps. Then they withdrew the arrows, and held them up to view as before with triumphant yelps, as if to say, 'So far have I swallowed it.' Sympathizers in the audience yelped in response. The next thing to be done was to apply the arrows to various parts of the patient's body. . . . This finished, the sick man and the buffalo robe were removed. The bear-

To know the reason for the type of costuming employed in this *alili* or show, it is necessary to recall the juncture in Dsilyi' Neyáni's supernatural experiences where the Butterfly woman cleansed the Navajo and adorned him in such manner "as the akáninili . . . is painted and ornamented to this day"—all preparatory to his visits to the abodes of the divine ones.

Speaking of the prophet and his supernatural guide, the myth relates, "They went to 'Valley-Surrounded-on-All-Sides-by-Hills' . . . where they found the house of the 'Holy Young Men,' of whom there were four. . . . A number of plumed arrows were hanging on the walls, and each young man (one standing in the east, one in the south, one in the west, and one in the north) held such an arrow in his extended right hand. . . . He [Dsilyi' Neyáni] was bidden to observe well how the holy young warriors stood, that he might imitate them in the rites he should establish amongst men."

And later—"They journeyed to 'Broad Cherry Trees,' where in a house of cherries with a door of lightning, there lived four gods named . . . 'Reared-within-the-Mountains' [the Prophet's patron gods, so to speak, in whose form the Butterfly Woman had recently molded him]. . . . Each held an arrow made of the cliff rose in his extended right hand. The head of the arrow was of stone, the fletching of eagle feathers, and the 'breath feather' of the downy plume of the Tsenáhale (Harpy of Navajo mythology). As they held the arrows they ejaculated, '*ai, ai, ai, ai,*'

. . . and, after the fourth *ai*, each one swallowed his arrow, head foremost, until the fletching touched his lips. Then he withdrew the arrow and they said, 'Thus do we wish the Navajo to do in the dance which you will teach them; but they must take good care not to break off the arrow-heads when they swallow and withdraw them.'"

In this dance is represented, in the person of the Yày-bi-chy, one of the premonitory experiences of the prophet Dsilyi' Neyáni during his captivity in a hostile Ute tribe, some time previous to his actual visits to the various abodes of the "divine ones." To quote from Dr. Matthew's record of the myth: "The pipes were lit and the council began. The talking in the strange tongue that he could not understand lasted long into the night, when he fancied that he heard the voice of the Yày-bi-chy above the din of the human voices, saying '*hu' hu' hu' hu''* in the far distance. He strained his attention and listened well and after awhile he felt certain that he heard the voice again nearer and louder. It was not long until the cry was repeated for the third time, and soon after the captive heard it once more loudly and distinctly, immediately to the west of the lodge. Then there was a sound as of footsteps at the door, and the white lightning entered at the smoke-hole and circled around the lodge, hanging over the heads of the council. But the Ute heard not the voice which the Navajo heard and saw not the vision he beheld. Soon the Yày-bi-chy entered the lodge and standing on the white lightning said: 'What is the matter with you, my grandchild? You take no thought about anything. Something you must do for yourself, or else, in the morning you will be whipped to death—that is what the council has decided.' Then the Yày-bi-chy

ers of the arrows danced once more around the fire and departed."

"Meanwhile in the songs of this rite, there is frequent reference to the plumed arrow [a most revered implement]. . . . All the other shows may be omitted at will, but this, it is said, must never be neglected."

Third Dance

"At 10 o'clock the sound of the whistle again called the spectators to attention and a line of twenty-three dancers came in sight. The one who led the procession bore in his hand a whizzer such as schoolboys use. . . . This he constantly whirled, producing a sound like that of a rain storm. After him came one who represented a character, . . . the Yàybichy, from the great nine days' ceremony of . . . the night chant, and he wore a blue buckskin mask that belongs to the character referred to. From time to time he gave the peculiar hoot or call of the Yàybichy, '*hu', hu', hu', hu'.*' After him followed eight wand-bearers. They were dressed like the bearers of the great plumed arrows; but instead of an arrow each bore a wand made of grass, cactus, and eagle plumes. The rest of the band were choristers in ordinary dress. As they were all proceeding around the fire for the fourth time, they halted in the west, the choristers sat and the wand-bearers formed a double row of four. Then the Yàybichy began to hoot, the orchestra to play, the choristers to sing, the whizzer to make his mimic storm, and the wand-bearers to dance. The latter keeping perfect time with the orchestra, went through a series of figures not unlike those of the modern quadrille. . . . When several of these evolutions had been performed in a graceful and orderly manner, the choristers rose, and all went singing out at the east."

gave the Navajo instructions as to how to escape and what valuable things to steal to take with him. Soon after this a sleep-bringing bird entered the lodge through the smoke-hole, hovering over the heads of the Ute. In a short time all were asleep, even the watch dogs, and the Navajo was free to carry out the instructions of the Yày-bi-chy and so begin the long series of trials and supernatural experiences."

There is one current myth which accounts for the origin of this dance in the following manner: "When Dsilyi' Neyáni visited the mountain of Bistcàgi, the home of *Estàn Cigini* (Holy Women), these divine beings had for ornaments on their walls the sun and the moon. When the great mythic dance was given they were among the guests. They brought their wall decorations, and when the time for their *alili* came, they wore the sun and the moon on their backs when they danced."

Fifth Dance

"It was after midnight when the blowing of a hoarse buffalo horn announced the approach of those who were to perform . . . the *tcòhanoai alili* or sun-show. There were twenty-four choristers and a rattler. There were two character dancers, who were arrayed . . . in little clothing and much paint. Their heads and arms were adorned with plumes of the war eagle, their necks with rich necklaces of genuine coral, their waists with valuable silver studded belts, and their loins with bright sashes of crimson silk. One bore on his back a round disk, nine inches in diameter, decorated with radiating eagle plumes to represent the sun. The other carried a disk, six and a half inches in diameter, similarly ornamented, to symbolize the moon. Each bore a skeleton wand of reeds that reminded one of the frame of a great kite; it was ornamented with pendant eagle plumes that swayed with every motion of the dancer. While the whole party was passing round the fire in the usual manner, wands were waved and heads bowed towards the flames. When it stopped in the west, the choristers sat and sang and the rattler stood and rattled while the bearers of the sun and moon danced at a lively rate for just three minutes. Then the choristers rose and they all sang and danced themselves out of sight."

The definite origin of this dance was not found recorded, though its presence in the modern exhibition may be accounted for in like manner as was the first dance, namely, an introduction by stranger guests, human or supernatural, at the first great mythic mountain chant, the one inaugurated for the sake of curing the prophet Dsilyi' Neyáni of his distaste for certain human conditions.

Ninth Dance

"It was after 1 o'clock in the morning when the dance of the *hoshkàwn* (*Yucca baccata*) began. The ceremony was conducted in the first part by twenty-two persons in ordinary dress. One bore, exposed to view, a natural root of yucca, crowned with its cluster of root leaves. . . . The rest bore in their hands wands of piñon. . . . On their third journey around the fire they halted in the west and formed a close circle for the purpose of concealing their operations. . . . After a minute spent in singing and many repetitions of '*Thohay*' [Stand], the circle opened, disclosing to our view the yucca róot planted in the sand. Again the circle closed; again the song, the rattle, and the chorus of '*Thohay*' were heard, and when the circle was opened the second time an excellent counterfeit of a small budding flower stalk was seen amid the fascicle of leaves. A third time the dancers formed their ring of occultation. After the song and din had continued for a few seconds, the circle parted for the third time, when, all out of season, the great panicle of creamy yucca flowers gleamed in the fire-light. The previous transformations of the yucca had been greeted with shouts and laughter; the blossoms were hailed with storms of applause. For the fourth and last time the circle closed, and when again it opened the blossoms had disappeared and the great, dark green fruit hung in abundance from the pedicels. When the last transformation was completed, the dancers went once more around the fire and departed, leaving the fruitful yucca behind them.

"In a moment after they had disappeared the form of one personating an aged, stupid, short-sighted, decrepit man was seen to emerge slowly from among the crowd of spectators in the east.

He was dressed in an old and woefully ragged suit and wore a high, pointed hat. His face was whitened and he bore a short crooked, wooden bow and a few crooked, ill-made arrows. His mere appearance provoked the stoic audience to screams of laughter, and his subsequent 'low comedy business' . . . failed not to meet with uproarious demonstrations of approval. Slowly advancing as he enacted his part, he in time reached the place where the yucca stood, and in his imbecile totterings, he at length stumbled on the plant and pretended to have his flesh lacerated by the sharp leaves. He gave a tremulous cry of pain, rubbed saliva on the part supposed to be wounded, and muttered his complaints in a weak and shaking voice. . . . At length, kneeling on the ground, with his face buried in the leaves, he feigned to discover it and rejoiced with querulous extravagance over his success. When he had marked the spot and the way back to it with an exaggerated burlesque of the Indian methods of doing things, he went off to find his 'old woman' . . . to pick the fruit. Soon he returned with a stalwart man, dressed to represent a hideous, absurd looking old granny," who played a skillful part in the somewhat coarse "low comedy" following.

Thus, at intervals, show followed show throughout the night, the fire-dance or fire-play coming as a culmination to the various exhibitions when the fire was fast dying out and the dawn was on the verge of breaking—"the most picturesque and startling of all," Dr. Matthews declares. But the *alilis* cited will suffice to illustrate how, out of the complexes of religious practices, definite dramatic conventions emerge. There is a certain conformity of dress to long-established rules, especially among the character impersonators; for instance, the paraphernalia of the actors in the Second Dance, the blue buck-skin mask of the Yàybichy in the Third Dance, the sun and moon disks worn by those playing the parts of the Estsàn Cigìni in the Fifth Dance. A sort of text is discernible in the conscientious attempt on the part of those presenting a show to adhere to long-established order of action in concert with perhaps even more accurately reproduced song accompaniment. The action itself, however, is not iron bound. There may be detected certain individual interpretations and innovations, the recognized license of every dramatic impersonator.

In these acted legends the greatest emphasis should be laid upon the Navajo's unmistakable employment of definite character parts. The moment the story side of the legend is lost sight of, in the objective, impersonal sense, and the moment the distinctly personal religious zeal and enthusiasm is lost sight of in the objectified, impersonal acting of a rôle, that moment the epic and lyric ingrains of a people's rudimentary literary consciousness is welded in the mean of dramatic expression. This stage has probably long been established among the Navajo as well as among the pueblo tribes. In serious performances the characters selected for impersonation, like the Greek characters in tragedy, are derived, not from the common ranks of men, but from gods or god-favored men. The deeds of this nobler typer of beings alone inspired the Indian audience. Thus, in the two *akáninilis* of the Second Dance may be discerned the semi-divine Dsilyi' Neyáni himself with one of his affiliated gods—one of those in whose likeness the Butterfly Woman molded the prophet. And in the strange actions and call of the Yàybichy may be recognized the personality of the good supernatural friend and guide of Dsilyi' Neyáni during his long series of hardships. In the Fifth Dance, nothing short of gods themselves, with little of the man occasioned interest such as is found in the Yàybichy is exhibited to the spectators in the rôles of the Estsàn Cigìni.

These are some of the characteristics of the serious drama present in Navajo exhibitions. But the Navajo, as well as the Hopi, had not only achieved a certain perfection in representations of this nature, but they had also progressed sufficiently beyond the sombre and awe-inspired stage of religious domination to allow of secular relaxation in the midst of the serious. The bit of low comedy Dr. Matthews described in part, coming at the close of the Ninth Dance, demonstrates this. It does not take a great reach of the imagination to recognize in this scene parts analogous to the rôles of Launcelot and Gobbo in the otherwise more or less tragic atmosphere of "The Merchant of Venice."

GREAT PLAINS RITUAL PERFORMANCES

From the more developed representations of pueblo peoples—developed, that is, from the standpoint of theatrical technique, especially in regard to scenic effects and recognized impersonations—let us turn to the less highly colored, purely religion-dominated, ceremonial of the great plains tribes. They cannot compete with the pueblo tribes in general standard of living perhaps; yet for all their cruder wandering, hunting life, in the profound moments of their religious expression, these plains tribes seem to strike an even more genuinely dramatic chord. With them, however, the human audience is of an entirely different sort. Though present at most ceremonials of a tribal nature, the tangible audience is little considered by those performing. With the exception of a privileged few, many of the religious pageants take into account only a divine audience. The resulting element of mystery, however, would seen to hold the more firmly the unquestionably sympathetic band of human spectators, so strong is the common bond of tribe and of religion. Be it of distinctly communal or individual purport, so long as a religious performance bears the stamp of tribal interest, this audience is assured. Thus is guaranteed to the great plains performances one of the inalienable essentials of dramatic art.

In all such ceremonials, symbolic ritual prevails. This is true of the largely communal observances, such as the Hako of the Pawnee; it is likewise true of the individual rites, such as those observed among the Omaha. As will be seen upon investigation, each of these two sets of rituals come close to the soul of man of any race and of any time. Both pertain to the dearest pledge of all mankind—the child, the desire and the hope of the individual as well as of the whole tribe. "The relation of parent to child," Mr. Mooney affirms, "brings out all the highest traits of Indian character." Hence, the two great ceremonials referred to, general as they are in practice among plains and eastern woodland peoples, have been fixed upon for illustrative purposes. The Hako was a wide-spread observance among plains Indians, indeed, wherever agriculture had gained a foothold, and certain features of the Omaha " rites of the individual " were common to most plains and eastern woodland folk.

THE PAWNEE HAKO[1]

The Hako, so called from certain of its sacred media, has a two-fold purpose: " First, to benefit certain individuals by bringing to them the promise of children, long life, and plenty; second, to affect the social relations of those who took part in it by establishing a bond between two distinct groups of persons belonging to different clans, gentes, or tribes, which was to insure between them friendship and peace." "The meaning flows from a fundamental human relationship, that of Father and Son, recognized in two forms, son-by-adoption and son-by-birth."

Such is the basic significance of the ceremonial as a whole, drawn from the Pawnee's conception of the universe and the relationship therein—the great and all-powerful Sky Father and the old and ever faithful Earth Mother, the Fathering Sun and the Corn Mother, upon all of whom the red men are as children dependent. In view of the universal significance, the Pawnee regulate the time of this observance—" in the spring, when the birds are mating," says the old Tahirussawichi, "or in the summer when the birds are nesting and caring for their young, or in the fall when the birds are flocking, but not in the winter when all things are asleep. With the Hako we are praying for the gift of life, of strength, of plenty, and of peace, so we must pray when life is stirring everywhere."

It is not necessary to follow up the details of the inauguration of the ceremonial and the period of symbolic preparation. Suffice

[1] According to the account obtained by Miss Fletcher from Tahirussawichi, a Pawnee priest and keeper of the Hako. See 22d *A. R. B. E.*, Part II, Washington, 1903. See, also, *Open Court,* 1913, Alexander, " The Mystery of Life."

it to say that it is within the power of a prominent chief to institute the Hako.   He becomes the Father, the leader of the Band of Fathers whom he selects.   From another tribe he chooses a chief to represent the Son, who in turn gathers together a Band of Children of whom he is the leader.   All are directed by the Kurahus or priest to whom has been intrusted the texts or methods of procedure during the entire ceremonial.   He is assisted by acolytes to whom he is teaching the rituals, and attended by two medicine men.   To translate these rôles in the terms of the classic Greek theater, the Kurahus, the director and ruling power of the whole production, would be recognized as the poet and chief actor; the two bands would be considered choric divisions, their separate leaders, by virtue of their prominence, being practically independent actors; the medicine men and acolytes, playing minor parts, would become servants and messengers.   The old man and the child, introduced for the first time in the secret ceremony, like the Kurahus, play principal rôles.   Not even the child, however, the central figure of the entire enactment, displaces the presiding priest in importance.   Throughout, the Kurahus remains the protagonist.

In the first stage of the Hako, the complete cast is not to be found.   Only the Father and his band, ever directed by the great high priest, take part, intently invoking the Son.   Not until after the symbol-enriched journey of the Fathers to the home of the Sons is the complete *dramatis personae* realized.   Now are met the necessary conditions for the central mystery, the dramatic enactment of the basic theme of the Hako.

At this point the two bands or choric divisions undergo the Greek complication of rôles, becoming at once both audience and actors.   Indeed, they constitute the sole understanding audience, favored as they are by previous instruction and brought within a thoroughly sympathetic and appreciative mood through profound prayer.   Now all is in readiness for the heart of the mystery; the sacred audience has been invoked and the human audience has been prepared.

The Hako Mystery[4]

This dramatization, the last of the three parts into which the ceremonial falls, comprises four acts or episodes of an exclusive nature together with an interlude of a public, social nature. The latter, coming between the last two episodes, serves to lighten the over-serious business of tragedy.

The ritual constituting the initial episode, is made up of three parts or situations. In the first place the Fathers "go seeking their child." This symbolic journey is directed to the home of the Son, where his little son or daughter may be found to play the part of Child. In the second situation the Powers are summoned to the child and the sacra are brought near him symbolic of giving him life and of promising to him children. After the Fathers have sung, "Come and fear not, my child, all is well," the Child takes four steps forward, symbolic of the progress of life, while the Fathers sing, "I am ready; come, my child." In the concluding situation of this introductory act, the Fathers, singing, "Behold your father walking with the child," set out for the ceremonial lodge in company with the Child.

The next ritual develops this subject matter in four situations, all concerned with the ceremonial preparation of the Child for the climactic consecration which occurs in the third episode. All that is done now is concealed from the view of the warriors in the two bands, for the business of war is not compatible with these rites. First the Child is symbolically cleansed for future life by water "come from Tirawa-atius," the father of all things. Symbolism is further carried out in regard to the bowl containing this sacred water—it is "shaped like the dome of the sky." An old man "chosen because of age and favors from powers above" is delegated to perform this rite that the Child may receive like blessings. First he touches the Child with the sacred water symbolic of the Sky Father, then with grass as a symbol of Earth Mother, giver of food to all. After this the old man anoints the Child with a mixture of red clay and sacred animal fat. Next he

[4] For accompanying songs, etc., see 22d *A. R. B. E.*, Part II, pp. 201–260, 345–362.

paints the Child's face with red paint, suggestive of the rising sun and symbolic of the vigor of life. This done, with blue paint he traces an arch about the forehead, the ends extending down each cheek, with a bridge across the nose—symbols of the arch of heaven and of the spirit paths from heaven to earth.

> "In these lines, we see the face of Tirawa-atius, giver of life and power to all things," says the old Tahirussawichi, later adding, "all who are to become leaders must be so painted."

In the last situation of this act, the old man fastens in the Child's hair, down from beneath the wing of the white eagle, suggestive of the breath and the life of the father of the child as well as of the breath of Tirawa-atius himself. Now the Child is told to look upon its reflection in the sacred water, running water being symbolic of a succession of generations. This done, a black covering is put over the Child's head—

> "that no one may look on the holy symbols. Only Tirawa-atius looks on them and knows all they mean. We do not look on them for they are holy."

In the third episode is reached the climax of the entire dramatic representation. First the Kurahus draws upon the ground a symbolic nest with his toe, thus imitating the eagle which builds its nest with its claws. There is, however, still greater significance in this act.

> "We are thinking of Tirawa making the world for the people to live in. . . . The circle . . . also represents the circle Tirawa-atius has made for the dwelling place of all the people."

Over this circle the Child is now held, its feet resting within the circumference. At this juncture an oriole's nest is secretly placed beneath the Child's feet, no one except the priest and the chief performing the act knowing what is being done under cover of the Child's robe. The oriole's nest is selected, because "Tirawa made the oriole build its nest so that no harm could come to it." Tobacco and bits of fat, " droppings that mark the trail made by hunters bringing meat home from the chase," are secretly placed in the nest. All this is to insure security and the good things of life not only to the Child, but to the whole generation which he represents.

> "The entire act means that the clan or tribe of the Son shall increase in peace and security in a land of fatness. This is the promise of Tirawa through the Hako."

A thank offering of sweet smoke brings this ritual to a close.

Now comes the public interlude, the part open to the intensely impressed, almost awe-stricken people outside.. Before the lodge the two bands, that of the Fathers and that of the Sons, perform a dance of thanks to song accompaniment. After this, gifts are distributed, exploits are recounted and sometimes acted out among the people themselves. Especially are battles dramatized at this time. The whole occasion is one of festivity and of good fellowship, a genuine respite from the overcharged atmosphere of the serious rituals. It serves to reinstate the world of reality.

After this, the prominent members of the Band of Fathers and of the Band of Sons, return to the lodge for the formal conclusion of the mystery play. Behind the holy place in the ceremonial lodge, a song of blessing is sung over the Child:

> "All that I have been doing to you, little child, has been a prayer to call down the breath of Tirawa-atius to give you long life and strength and to teach you that you belong to him, that you are his child."

The Child is now unveiled, the symbolic paint removed and all the articles employed in the ceremony made into rolls to be presented to the Son. Then the Father addresses the Son. When he has finished speaking, he puts the bundle in the arms of the Child and leads it back to its father, the Son. The latter receives the offering, and " the child runs off to play." Shortly after this the Sons also withdraw and the Fathers are left alone to make a final distribution of gifts, the concluding feature of the entire Hako.

Such is the substance of the Pawnee religious drama as embodied in the Hako. In frankly designating it a drama, we do not presume too much. The underlying theme is of universal significance. It is developed clearly and in a dramatically unified manner, growing steadily to a climax or turning point, the pure religious exaltation of which gives promise of the joyous calm achieved in the final act. In point of fact, the Hako mystery meets the basic requisites of the five act drama, for, after all, from the standpoint of dramatic technique, the public interlude itself is an organic part of the drama proper. Following the third ritual, it fulfills the true function of a fourth act, "the period of preparation," essential to any serious drama. The joyous nature of this public performance forestalls more definitely the happy ending, promised in the third ritual.

The Hako mystery presents by analogy a strange complex of the Shakespearean drama and the classic Greek tragedy. The impersonal nature of the subject matter is suggestive of both, though the concentrated nature of the situation is more indicative of the Greek. Again, the typically climactic nature of the third episode is characteristic of both the Greek and the Shakespearean drama. But the five stages of theme progress as designated by rituals, coincides with Shakespeare's dramatic form. The absolute attention to the unified development of abstract idea in action at the expense of any individual character development, points to the Greek way of doing things. The nature of the two choruses with their respective leaders, the scarcity of qualified actors would seem to establish this Greek analogy, were it not for the typically Shakespearean psychology evinced in the fourth act, in which man is brought back to earth and human relations reëstablished. The religious awe surrounding the central mystery of the oriole's nest is strongly suggestive of the atmosphere of awe and religious exaltation enshrouding the supernatural end of the Œdipus in Sophocles' "Œdipus at Colonos." It is not necessary to go back to the Eleusinean mysteries for this analogy. The Greek tragedy as a finished art affords it. The final act would seem to bear out this judgment, leaving the abiding calm and tranquility of a wholly clarifying and satisfying solution, such as the Greek tragedy produced, as did Shakespeare too in the last period of his writings. "We are always happy when we are with the Hako," says Tahirussawichi. Is it necessary to establish further the inherent dramatic significance of the central mystery in the Hako?

OMAHA RITES PERTAINING TO THE INDIVIDUAL

Closely allied to the *passion-purging*, soul-exalting effect of the Hako are the more distinctly individual ceremonials of the peace-loving Omaha.[5] Here, too, the child is the ruling motif, first as an infant of eight days, then as a child of three or more, and finally as a youth or maid.

Introduction of the Child to the Cosmos

Until its ritualistic recognition, the newborn babe was but an element of the universe "through the bond of the common life-giving power," with no human significance, with no tribal or gens connection. Not until eight days after its birth was the Omaha child formally introduced into the "teeming life of the universe." The priest, with whom this function was hereditary, having been summoned, took his stand at the door of the tent where the baby lay, and raising his hand palm outwards towards the sky, chanted in a loud tone a supplication to the "powers of the heavens, the air, and the earth" for the protection of the child, as it should travel "the rugged road, stretching over four hills"—infancy, youth, manhood, and old age. Here are sounded.

> "the emotions of the human soul, touched with the love of off-spring, alone with the might of nature, and companioned only by the living creatures whose friendliness must be sought if life is to be secure on its journey."

Meanwhile, the baby life is further protected by a tiny hole cut in the sole of one of its first moccasins.

> "This is done in order that if a messenger from the spirit world should come and say to the child, 'I have come for you'; the

[5] See 27th *A. R. B. E.*, Washington, 1905–1906, pp. 119–128.

child could answer, 'I cannot go on a journey—my moccasins are worn out!'"

And so the child is left free to grow, after its introduction to the universe, until it can walk steadily by itself. At this stage are enacted the dramatic rites in which the child is "symbolically sent into the midst of the winds" for further insurance of life and of health.

Introduction of the Child into the Tribe

At best the account of these rituals is incomplete. The greater part of what is recorded of the two secret mystery plays constituting this ceremonial comes from what a boyhood friend of Joseph La Flesche was able to hear and remember while hiding in the ceremonial tent. And yet what remains is worth considering.

In the spring, after the first thunders had been heard, when the grass was green and the meadow lark was singing, the herald went about the Húthuga (tribal circle), announcing that the time was at hand for the second set of childhood ceremonies. A tent was set up and made sacred, within which the prescribed rites were to be performed by priests whose hereditary duty it was. These secret performances were witnessed from the east-facing doorway by a company of intense spectators; for, having to do with the making of the child a distinctly human being with recognized name and place in gens and tribe, these ceremonials were of profound interest, not only to parents with children of the essential stage of development but to every true clansman and tribesman as well. The child, as the individual representative of tribal increase and prosperity, was of vital importance—hence, the human audience, hungrily gathering up what scraps they could from the two secret enactments, directed primarily to the god of Thunder, the controller of human life. Only for the little boy, however, were the two ceremonials performed, "The Turning of the Child" and "To-Cut-the-Hair." In the case of the little girls the second observance was omitted, for reasons that will be made clear later.

"Turning-the-Child"

The mother and the father bring the little boy to the sacred tent. The mother leading him to the entrance thronged with spectators, is met by the priest whom she addresses:

> "Venerable man, I desire my child to wear moccasins." Then, as she presents the priest with gifts she has brought as fees, "I desire my child to walk long upon the earth; I desire him to be content with the light of many days. We seek your protection. We hold to you for strength."

Then the priest replies, addressing the child:

> "You shall reach the fourth hill sighing. You shall be bowed over; you shall have wrinkles, your staff shall bend under your weight. I speak to you that you may be strong." Then, with his hand on the child's shoulder, "What you have brought me shall not be lost to you; you shall live long and enjoy many possessions; your eyes shall be satisfied with many good things."

So concludes the introductory part of the ceremony, the only part fully comprehended by the onlookers. At this point the priest conducts the child, carrying his new moccasins, to the center of the tent where the mystery proper is enacted. A fire is burning here,

> "the flames typical of the life-giving power . . ., an aid toward insuring the capacity for a long, fruitful, and successful life in the tribe."

On the east side of the fireplace is a stone, emblematic of long life upon the earth and of the wisdom of age; to the west of the fireplace is a ball of grass, the symbolic meaning of which remains obscure.

When the priest reaches the fireplace, he assumes the rôle of the Thunder God, whose priest he is,—"I am a powerful being; I breathe from my lips over you." Then, as priest again, he sings the invocation to the Winds:

> "Ye four come hither and stand, near shall ye stand,
> In four groups shall ye stand,
> Here shall ye stand, in this place stand."
>   *(The Thunder rolls.)*

406

At the close of this song the priest faces the child towards the east. Then lifting the little boy by the shoulders, he holds him over the stone on which his feet are allowed to rest. Thus is begun the all-important act of turning the child from left to right, lifted by the shoulders each time and so faced south, then west, north, and back to the east during the singing of the ceremonial song:

> "Turned by the winds goes the one I send yonder;
> Yonder he goes who is whirled by the winds;
> Goes where the four hills are standing;
> There, in the midst of the winds do I send him,
> Into the midst of the winds, standing there."

(The Thunder rolls.)

All this is performed with the greatest caution on the part of the priest. It is a period of intensely dramatic significance; for the audience is fully aware of the fatality of any flaw in the execution of this act. Should the child by any bad chance struggle and turn even a trifle in the wrong direction, all the spectators with one voice raise a cry of alarm. To them such an occurrence is as indicative of disaster as is the best wrought out climax in the art tragedy bodeful of the inevitable end, to an esthetic audience of civilized folk.

At the close of this scene, the priest puts the new whole moccasins on the child's feet, singing the while:

> "Here unto you has been spoken the truth;
> Because of this truth you shall stand.
> Here declared is the truth.
> Here in this place has been shown you the truth.
> Therefore, arise! go forth in its strength!"

(The Thunder rolls.)

With the last verse the child is set on its feet and made to take four steps, symbolic of its entrance upon the journey of life. Its baby name is thrown away and its *nikie* (elk or buffalo, etc.) assumed. In conclusion, the priest instructs the child in regard to

467

certain religious rites of his gens, which he must observe, together with the penalties attached to their violation.

Wé bashna or " To-Cut-the-Hair "

So ends the first ritual, but for the boy there is still another observance. Destined to become a warrior—and every Omaha man must fit himself to defend home and tribe—the boy's life is further consecrated to Thunder, as the god of war, by another priest whose special duty it is.

Leading the boy to the west side of the fire, the officiating priest faces him towards the east. He selects a lock of hair from the crown of the boy's head, ties it, and cuts it off, laying it away in a sacred case. As he performs this act, he sings,—

> " Grandfather ! far above on high,
> The hair like a shadow passes before you.
> Grandfather ! far above on high,
> Dark like a shadow the hair sweeps before you into the midst of
>   your realm,"

The severing of the lock, a potent determiner of life and death in the Indian mind, implies the consecration of the boy's life to Thunder, the power controlling the warrior's destiny. Symbolically this hair-offering with all its vital significance is sent to the Thunder God, who in the following song is represented as accepting the life pledge to him and as declaring his determination to do with it as he pleases:

> " What time I will, then only then,
> A man lies dead, a gruesome thing,
> What time I will, then suddenly
>
> .   .   .   . etc.
> Like a shadow dark the man shall lie,"

What else may occur before the final song, is not recorded. The concluding chant, however, is an invocation to the flames, the third of the cosmic forces according to the Omaha :

> " Come hither, haste to help me,
> Ye flames, ye flames, O come !

> O red-hot fire, hasten!
> O haste, ye flames, to come.
> . . . . etc.
> Come hither, haste to help me!"

The position and exact part played by the orchestra or chorus, as the case may be, remain obscure. Yet, fragments enough have been saved from the wreck of this drama-wrought religious observance to bear unmistakable marks of the great play of life and death, in which the responsibility-burdened child represents mankind. Each priest furnishes a dual dramatic character. At one moment he is the god himself, at the next, only the delegated representative of the god. He acts directly each rôle, speaking in the capacity of each character. Taken in connection with the sympathetic, if not wholly understanding audience, these internal features of mimetic action coupled with dialogue are sufficient to establish dramatic elements in these particular rites.

Introduction to Individual Life and to the Supernatural

Noń Zhin Zhon or "To-Stand-Sleeping"

In the third stage of individual rites, the Omaha youth was introduced "to the individual life and the supernatural." The consciousness of self, awakened at puberty, the time at which the mind of the child "becomes white," as the Omaha say, was closely associated with a consciousness of a highly spiritual, impersonal sort.

This rite also took place in the spring. But it allowed of no audience, that is no human audience; it provided for little specific impersonation. Strictly speaking, in itself, this ceremonial presents few dramatic features; yet, in the inviolable vows made during this rite, there are ingrained dramatic possibilities of profound nature. The rite itself is purely and intensely religious.

When he is "old enough to know sorrow," the Omaha youth with his face covered with soft clay, a symbol of humility, perhaps, sets out alone for the hills to enter upon a fasting vigil of four days. As he is leaving home, the youth's father puts into his hands a bow and arrow; but these he is forbidden to use, no matter how hungry he may become. Their function is to teach him the powerful lesson of endurance and self-restraint. During this time, he must pray for strength to Wakon da, "the great power," not to the lesser powers such as the sun, the moon, the stars, or the earth. This prayer is an "appeal for help throughout life."

> "You are to go forth to cry to Wakon' da—'Wakon' da! here, needy he stands and I am he,'" the Sacred Legend enjoins. "When on the hills, you shall not ask for any particular thing. The answer may not come to you as you expect; whatever is good, that may Wakon' da give."

At the end of the four days, as a final supplication, the youth must "wipe his tears with the palms of his hands and lift his wet hands to the sky, then lay them to the earth."

This much of the symbolic rôle, that must be played at least once by every Omaha youth and may be performed by any Omaha maid, is all that need be cited here. The fatal import of the sacred vow, made upon this occasion, constitutes its chief dramatic significance. Were an audience present at this realistically symbolic trial of man, a parallel might be drawn between it and the morality play of "Every Man." But this audience is not present. The vow, however, is made all the more terribly binding, perhaps, on account of the absence of human witnesses.

In the light of the Omaha rites of the individual, especially the consecration of the life of the boy to Thunder together with the later period of prayer and pledge on the lonely hills, turn to Miss Fletcher's account of "The Mother's Vow."[6] This is a Dakota story; but the close blood relation and common religious practices of the Omaha and the Dakota make this application entirely feasible.

> "In the early part of the century a Dakota woman fasted and prayed, and Thunder came to her in her vision. To the god she promised to give her first-born child. When she became a mother she forgot in her joy that the life of her little one did not belong to her; nor did she recall her fateful vow until one bright spring day, when the clouds gathered

[6] See Fletcher, *Indian Story and Song from North America.*

and she heard the roll of the thunder,—a sound which summoned all persons consecrated to this god to bring their offerings and to pay their vows. Then she remembered what she had promised; but her heart forbade her to lay the infant, which was smiling in her arms, upon the cloud-swept hill-top. She pressed the baby to her breast, and waited in silence the passing of the god in the storm.

"The following spring, when the first thunder pealed, she did not forget her vow; but she could not gather strength to fulfill it.

"Another year passed, and again the thunder sounded. Taking the toddling child by the hand, the mother climbed the hill; and, when the top was reached, she placed it on the ground and fled. But the boy scrambled up and ran after her, and his frightened cry stayed her feet. He caught her garments and clung to them; and although the thunder called, she could not obey. Her vow had been made before she knew the strength of a mother's love.

"Gathering the boy into her arms, she hid herself and him from the presence of the god. The storm passed, and the mother and child returned to the lodge; but fear had taken possession of her, and she watched her son with eyes in which terror and love struggled for the mastery.

"One day, as the little one played beside a rippling brook, laughing and singing in his glee, suddenly the clouds gathered, the flashing lightning and crashing thunder sent beast and bird to cover, and drove the mother out to find her child. She heard his voice above the fury of the storm, calling to her. As she neared the brook, a vivid flash blinded her eyes. For a moment she was stunned; but, recovering, she pushed on, only to be appalled by the sight that met her gaze. Her boy lay dead. The thunder god had claimed his own.

"No other children came to lighten the sorrow of the lonely woman; and every spring, when the first thunder sounded, and whenever the storm swept the land, this stricken woman climbed the hills, and there standing alone, facing the black rolling clouds, she sang her song of sorrow and of fealty:—

> Edho he! [7]
> "Behold! on their mighty pinions flying,
> They come, the gods come once more
> Sweeping o'er the land,
> Sounding their call to me, to me their own.
> Wa-gi-un![8] Ye on mighty pinions flying,
> Look on me here, me your own,
> Thinking on my vow
> As ye return once more, Wa-gi-un!"

[7] Sighing vocables.

[8] Dakota term for the thunder bird.

Could there be a more dramatic application of these sacred rites, a more absolute instance of tragedy, terrible and inevitable?

> "The essence of tragedy," Mr. Courteney[9] declares, "is always a conflict between a great law or power, universal or world wide in its scope, and the free will of the individual."

Such is the pitiable plight of the Dakota mother. On the one side comes the deep and irresistible call of a mother's love; on the other, the even more compelling demand of a divine power. The frail human resistance against this moral force is hopeless, utterly hopeless, yet that resistance must be made, so ingrained in the soul is parental love. The hapless Dakota mother is caught in the toils of fate quite as inextricably as ever was Antigone.

This dramatic material, grounded upon religious integrity, presents a typical Greek situation. The tragic incident, involving those "near and dear to one another,"[10] "through pity and fear effecting the proper purgation of these emotions,"[11] further establishes the Greek analogy. This theme is not suited to the less avowedly moral treatment of the romanticist. The grand, superhuman acceptance of the decree of fate, ringing out in the self-restraint-exalted song of the god-punished mother is indicative of a calm of the highest and most philosophical order. There is none of the complaint, none of the undying rebellion of the individual against divine ruling. No more is there the conciliatory note of the Christian heaven, where all is at last righted. In the truly Greek spirit, the inevitable is accepted, calmly and bravely, in full accord with moral order and there is an end to it.[12]

And yet, for all its Greek conception, M. Stopfer[13] would probably agree that Shakespeare's dramatic scheme[14] is best adapted to its development. Several years are involved in the plot, change of place is necessitated, and truly Shakespearean growth

---

[9] Courteney, *The Idea of Tragedy in Ancient and Modern Drama*, 1900.
[10] Aristotle's *Poetics*, XIV, Butcher translation.
[11] Aristotle's *Poetics*, VI, Butcher translation.
[12] See Frye, *Corneille: the Neo-classic Tragedy and the Greek*, Sec. II.
[13] Stopfer, *Shakespeare et les Tragiques Grecs*.
[14] Sherman, *What Is Shakespeare?* 1902.

of character is needed to give this tragic material its greatest force.   This need not, however, impair the all pervading spirit of Greek acceptance of divine ruling.   From the fateful Thunder God's "What time I will . . . a man lies dead," etc., to the intensely religious calm of the desolate mother "thinking on her vow," the Æschylean moral order prevails.

* * *

By no means does this limited survey exhaust the dramatic possibilities of the pueblo, great plains, and eastern woodland religious ceremonials.   The latter alone, for all their early contact with Christian peoples, retain not a few untainted religious practices of a dramatic nature.   The various medicine societies,[1] perhaps the most widespread of all Indian institutions, afford an almost endless source of investigation.   And closely allied to and compounded with the medicine cults, the far reaching religious festival called the Sun Dance[2] offers considerable dramatic material.   Fundamentally a religious observance, it was also a social occasion for epic recitals of the glorious deeds of dead warriors and realistic enactments of by-gone battles, in which there was as patriotic assurance of race supremacy as the "Gorboduc" itself afforded.   The dramatic enactment of battles was an important feature of the Omaha Sacred Pole[3] observance, at the ordination of which the people said:

> "Let us appoint a time when we shall again paint him [the Sacred Pole] and *act before him the battles we have fought.*"

That the same dramatic institution was characteristic of the Pawnee has already been seen in connection with the Hako.   Even

[1] See 7th *A. R. B. E.*, Washington, 1892, "The Midéwiwin of the Ojibwa" and *Jour. Am. Folk Lore,* April–June, 1911, "The Ritual of the Winnebago Medicine Dance." etc.

[2] IV Anthrop.   Series Field Columbian Mus., 1903, "Arapaho Sun Dance"; 11th *A. R. B. E.*, Washington, 1890, "A Study of Siouan Cults," p. 450.

[3] See 27th *A. R. B. E.*, Washington, 1906, p. 217.

one of the latest religious cults, the Ghost Dance,[4] permeated
with Christian lore, evinces much dramatic material purely Indian
in conception.   But further citations are not needed.

It is not to be maintained that every Indian ritual shows evi-
dences of the high and of the noble, qualities beautiful and in-
spiring.   Like certain Greek religious practices, Indian ceremonials are at times characterized by the base and the irreconcilably
terrible.   In Greek literary records, however, these features were,
for the most part, ignored; and so should they be in the attempt
to discover literary values in Indian rituals.   As a judgment on
life, life idealized and made worth living, literature should reflect
the best thoughts, the best emotions of which a people is capable.
Matthew Arnold[5] says:

> " The critical power . . . tends . . . to make the best ideas pre-
> vail."   And again, the business of criticism is *" a disinterested en-
> deavor to learn and propagate the best that is known and thought
> in the world,* and thus to establish a current of fresh and true
> ideas."

In following out this program, it is not necessary to fall into the
common error of enthusiasts.

> " There is a curious tendency," Dr. Powell[6] remarks, " observable
> in students to overlook aboriginal vices and to exaggerate aborigi-
> nal virtues."

After all the Indian is merely a savage.   The low and the base
exist even in his religious practices, to be sure; yet towering far
above these ignoble features are idealistic conceptions.   In the
end, it is the idealizations of which a people is capable, that sur-
vive, those finer thoughts that make possible the exalted life as
distinguished from mere physical existence.   Such literary quali-

---

[4] See 11th *A. R. B. E.*, Washington, 1890, " A Study of Siouan Cults,"
p. 484; 14th *A. R. B. E.*, Washington, 1896, " Ghost Dance Religion."
   [5] Arnold, *On the Function of Criticism.*
   [6] See 7th *A. R. B. E.*, Washington, 1886, " Indian Linguistic Families of
North America."

ties, from a dramatic standpoint at least, the pueblo and plains Indians possessed.   Whether they could ever have embodied their crude material into any worthy literary form according to European standards, is another problem.   Certainly the soul of a worthy literature shines through the beautiful poetic imagery of not a few of their religious dramatizations.